Military Tech

MILITARY AIRCRAFT

JULIA GARSTECKI

BLACK RABBIT BOOKS

Bolt is published by Black Rabbit Books
P.O. Box 3263, Mankato, Minnesota, 56002.
www.blackrabbitbooks.com

Jennifer Besel, editor; Michael Sellner, designer;
Omay Ayres, photo researcher

Library of Congress Cataloging-in-Publication Data
Names: Garstecki, Julia, author.
Title: Military aircraft / by Julia Garstecki.
Description: Mankato, Minnesota : Black Rabbit Books, [2018] | Series: Bolt. Military tech | Includes bibliographical references and index. | Audience: Grades 4-6. | Audience: Ages 9-12.
Identifiers: LCCN 2016049965 (print) | LCCN 2016050298 (ebook) | ISBN 9781680721621 (library binding) | ISBN 9781680722260 (e-book)
Subjects: LCSH: Airplanes, Military–Juvenile literature. | Military helicopters–Juvenile literature.
Classification: LCC UG1243 .G37 2018 (print) | LCC UG1243 (ebook) | DDC 623.74/6-dc23
LC record available at https://lccn.loc.gov/2016049965

Printed in the United States at CG Book Printers,
North Mankato, Minnesota, 56003. 3/17

Image Credits

Alamy: 508 collection, 13 (bottom); Stocktrek Images, 22 (top); US Air Force Photo, 20; US Marines Photo, Cover; Associated Press: AP, 18–19 (background); http://www.af.mil/News/Photos: US Air Force Photo, 1, 28–29, Back Cover; Shutterstock: 3000ad, 26–27; Andy Dean Photography, 27; Artem Anikeyev, 13 (top); Brian Goff, 18 (Tu-160); Jaroslav Moravcik, 3, 32; MyImages - Micha, 24; Peter R Foster IDMA, 8–9, 14, 31; Ranga Yogeshwalka, 18 (B-2), 19 (B-52); Timonf, 18 (F-16), 19; Vladimir Sazonov, 22 (bottom); Wikipedia Commons: Toshiro Aoki (www.jp-spotters.com, 25 (top); Unknown, 10–11, 16–17 (all), 19 (Eurofighter), 21, 25; U.S. Air Force - SSgt Eric Harris, 6; U.S. Air Force - Staff Sgt. Christopher Boitz, 4–5; www.jsf.mil, 19 (F-35); XaHyMaH, 19 (T-50)

CONTENTS

CHAPTER 1

In the ACTION

Two F-16 fighters race through the air. They move at 1,500 miles (2,414 kilometers) per hour. The crews fire the planes' weapons. They hit an enemy airplane and it explodes. The F-16s fly away to fight again.

RESCUE
290
SSGT DONALD LEWIS
A1C WILLIAM SMITH
1 PUSH BUTTON TO OPEN DOOR
2 PULL RING OUT 6 FEET TO
JETTISON CANOPY
SN1416
63

Weapons of F-16 Fighters
AMRAAM guided missile
AIM-9M heat-seeking missile
M61A1 Vulcan Gatling gun
miles 0 5
weapon's maximum distance

Amazing Aircraft

Aircraft are important to many militaries. Fighters, bombers, and **drones** fly over enemy lands. They carry soldiers and supplies. And their high-tech features are amazing.

COUNTRIES WITH LARGEST NUMBER OF MILITARY AIRCRAFT

through 2015

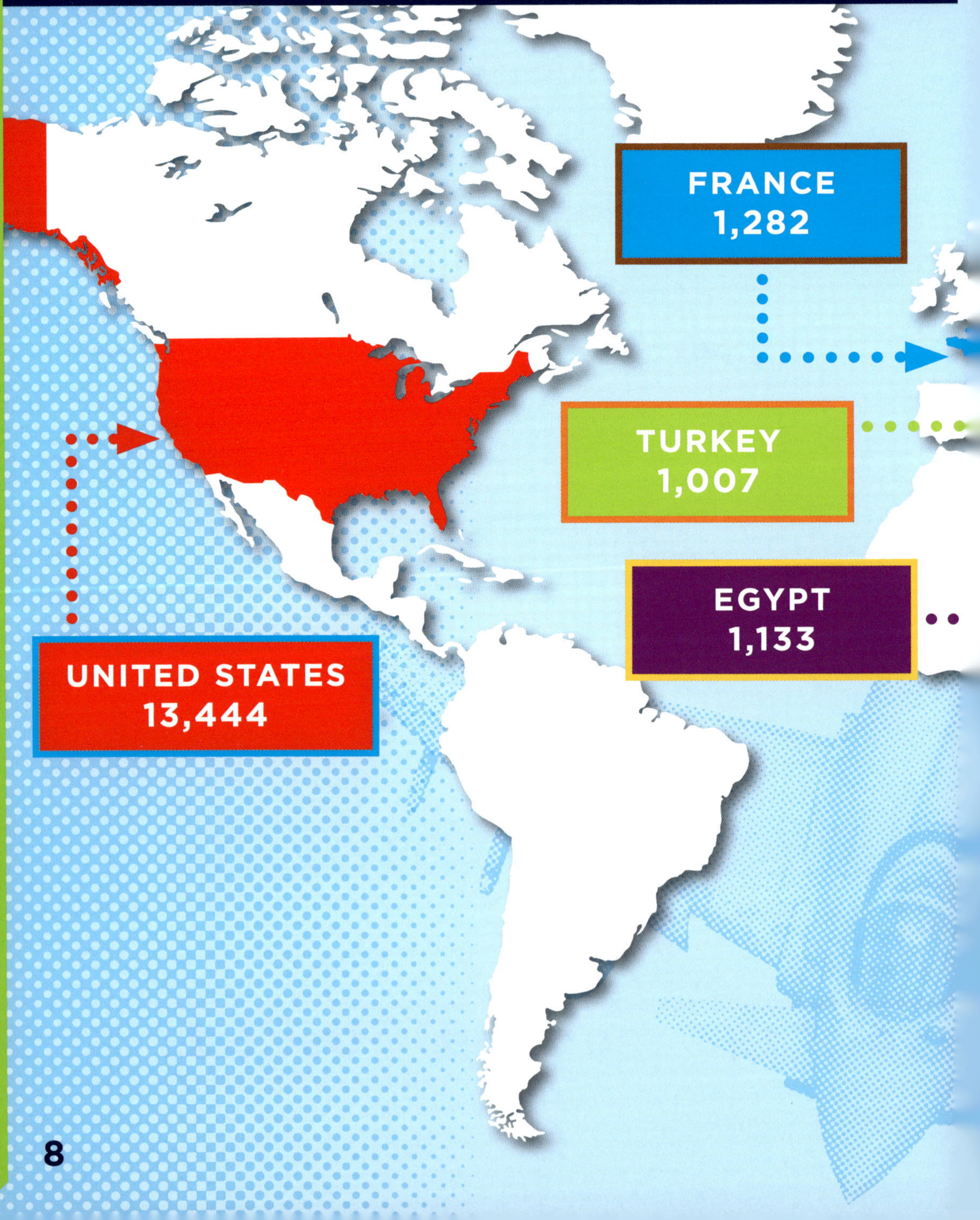

RUSSIA
3,547
NORTH KOREA
944
SOUTH KOREA
1,451
INDIA
2,086
CHINA
2,942
JAPAN
1,590

CHAPTER 2

MILITARY

Bombers and Fighters

Bombers are large military planes. Pilots fly them up high. Then crews bomb targets below.

B-2 BASICS → flies up to 630 miles (1,014 km) per hour

The B-2 Spirit is the most expensive aircraft in the world. It can bomb a target without being seen. A special **coating** hides the plane from enemies.

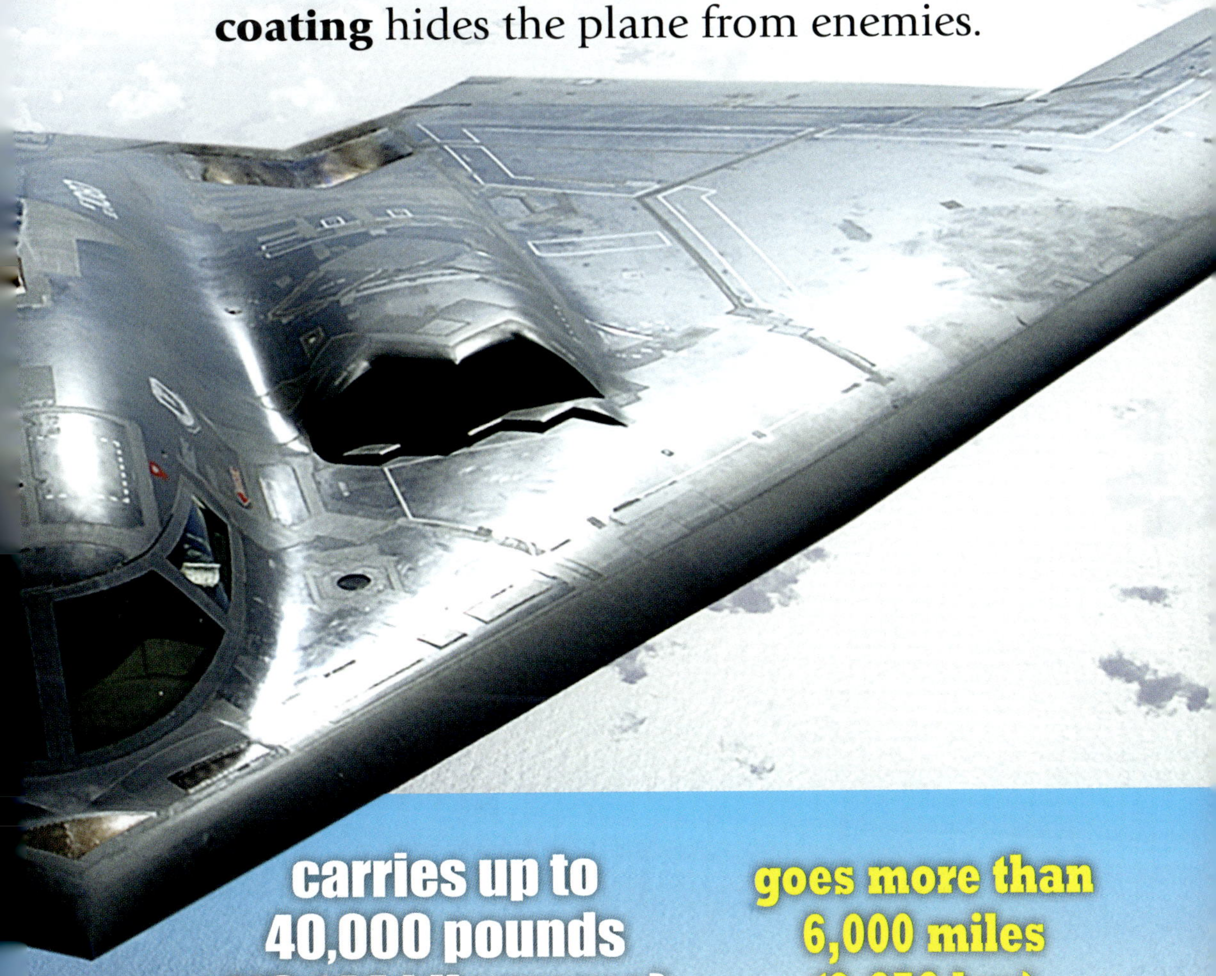

carries up to 40,000 pounds (18,144 kilograms) of weapons

goes more than 6,000 miles (9,656 km) without refueling

Heavyweights

The Tu-160 is the world's largest bomber. It is also the heaviest. Even though it's big, it's fast. The Tu-160 can climb 230 feet (70 meters) per second.

The B-52 is perfect for long **missions**. It can fly for more than 30 hours nonstop. And it can carry 70,000 pounds (31,751 kg) of weapons.

B-52 ALL THE WEAPONS IT CAN CARRY AT ONCE

НОВИКОВ

Eurofighter Typhoon

Fighters protect bombers on missions. They also attack enemies on the ground.

The Eurofighter Typhoon's top speed is more than 1,500 miles (2,414 km) per hour. A computer moves the wings. A person can't move them fast enough.

Countries that Use or Have Ordered Typhoons

(through 2016)

- Austria
- Germany
- Italy
- Oman
- Saudi Arabia
- Spain
- United Kingdom

New Stealth Fighters

Companies are working on new **stealth** fighters. These planes have amazing technology.

The T-50 PAK FA is a Russian fighter. It turns easily at **supersonic** speeds.

The F-35 is a U.S. fighter. It will be almost impossible to spot with **radar**.

It costs at least $50 million to make a T-50.

COMPARING FIGHTERS' AND BOMBERS' SPEEDS

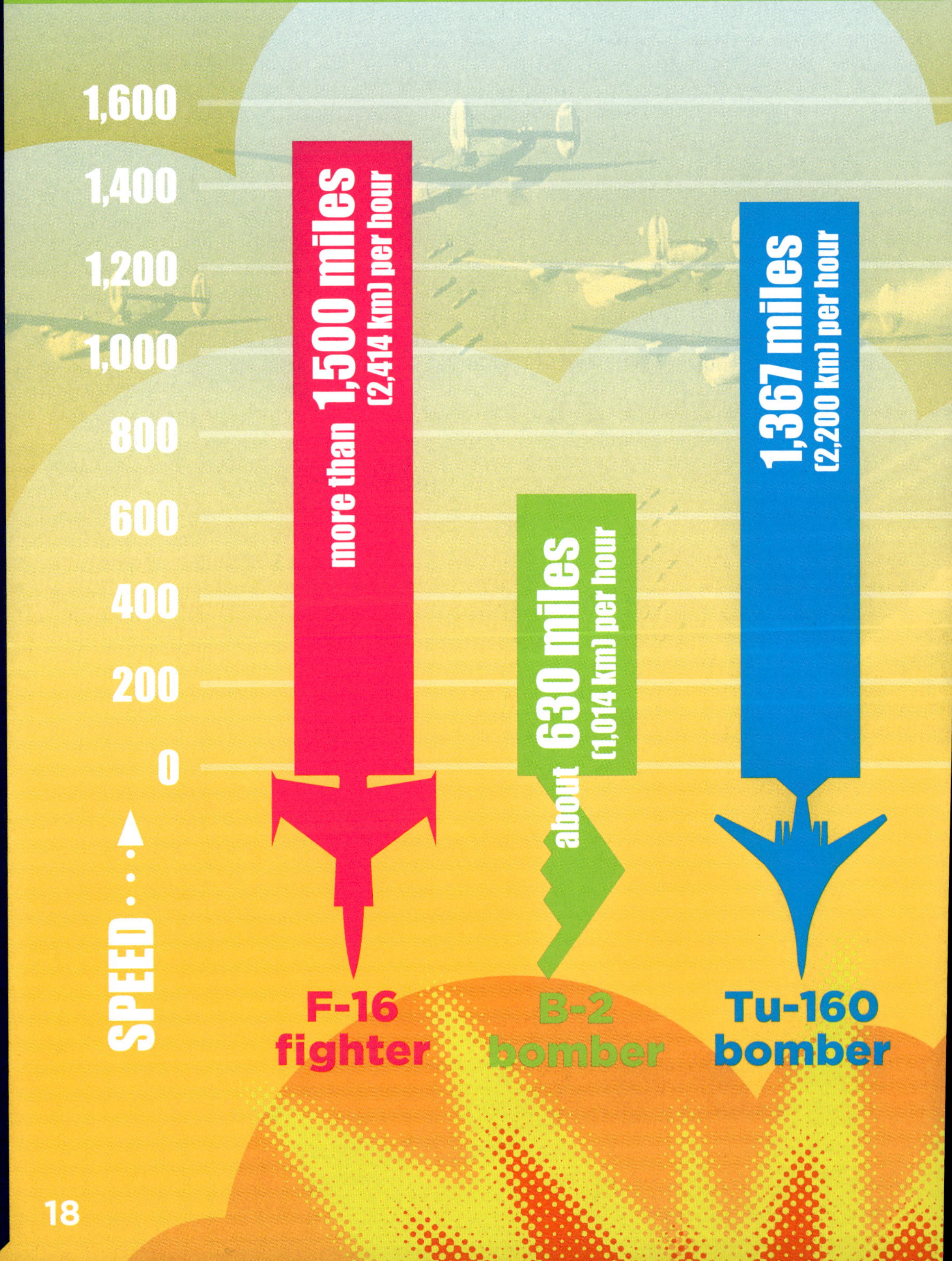

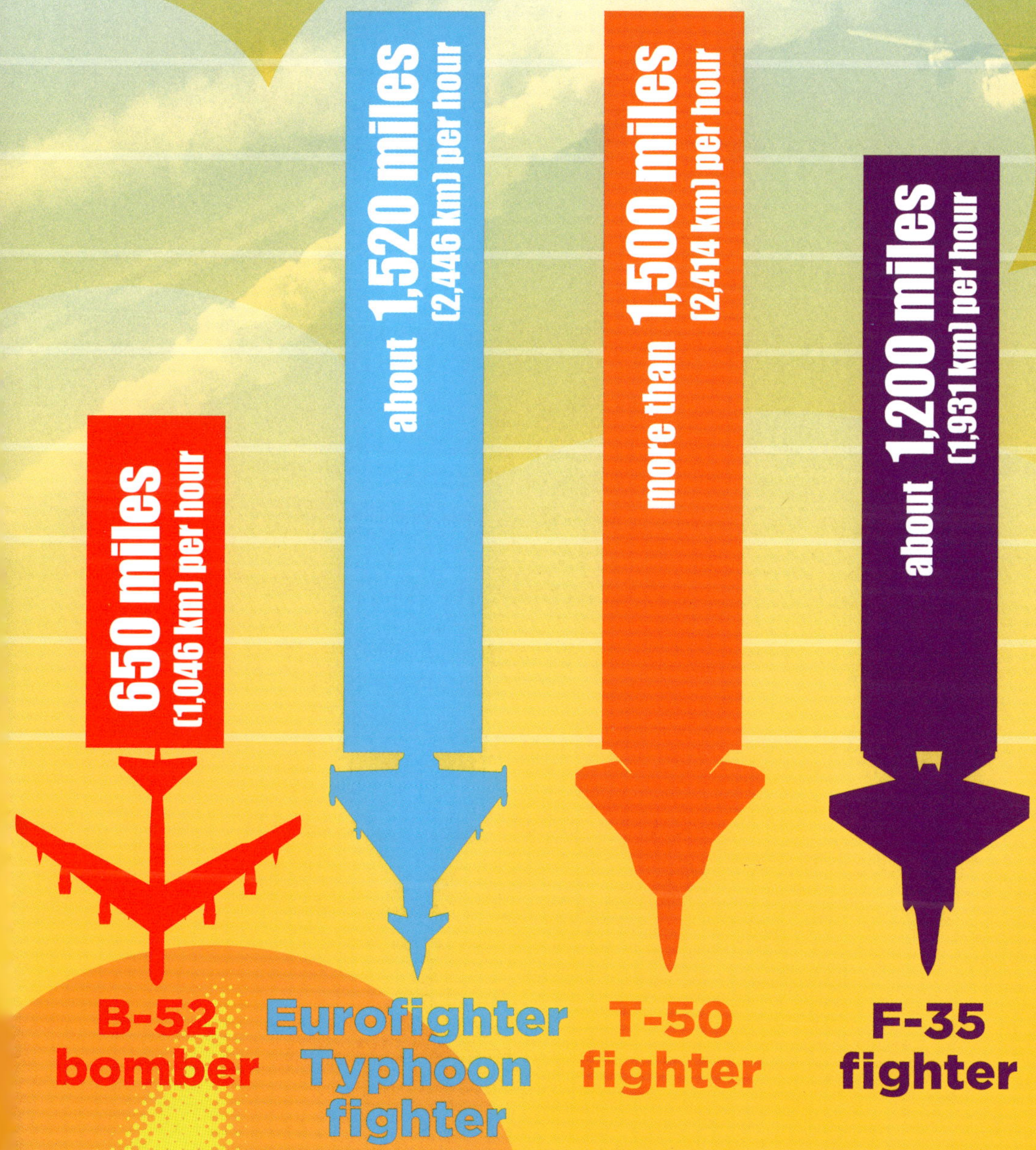
650 miles
(1,046 km) per hour
B-52 bomber
about 1,520 miles
(2,446 km) per hour
Eurofighter Typhoon fighter
more than 1,500 miles
(2,414 km) per hour
T-50 fighter
about 1,200 miles
(1,931 km) per hour
F-35 fighter

CHAPTER 3

Military HELICOPTERS

Helicopters move soldiers and supplies. They also rescue soldiers in trouble.

The V-22 Osprey is part helicopter and part plane. It takes off like a helicopter. The **rotors** change position in the air. Then it flies like an airplane.

A crew of four people flies the Osprey.

Attack Helicopters

The AH-64 Apache was built for war. If hit near the gas tank, parts swell up. They shut the hole to keep gas from leaking.

The Kamov Ka-50 Black Shark is one of the fastest attack helicopters. Its rotors spin in opposite directions. This spinning makes the chopper **stable** and fast.

MILITARY HELICOPTERS

By the Numbers

Ka-50 Black Shark

MAXIMUM WEIGHT AT TAKEOFF
23,810 pounds
(10,800 kg)

TOP SPEED
about **300 miles**
(483 km) per hour

AH-64 APACHE

MAXIMUM WEIGHT AT TAKEOFF
15,075 pounds
(6,838 kg)

TOP SPEED
173 miles
(278 km) per hour

V-22 OSPREY

MAXIMUM WEIGHT AT TAKEOFF
52,600 pounds
(23,859 kg)

TOP SPEED
311 miles
(501 km) per hour

CHAPTER 4

Looking to the FUTURE

New technology will change future aircraft. Militaries will use more drones. Scientists are working on a new material too. If a plane is shot, this material will heal itself.

SERIAL #:
PN:
SW:
DATE:
DANGER
DRONE CAMERA

AIRCRAFT COSTS

Always Changing

Aircraft are important to militaries. They move people quickly. And they carry powerful weapons. New technology will make them safer and even more amazing.

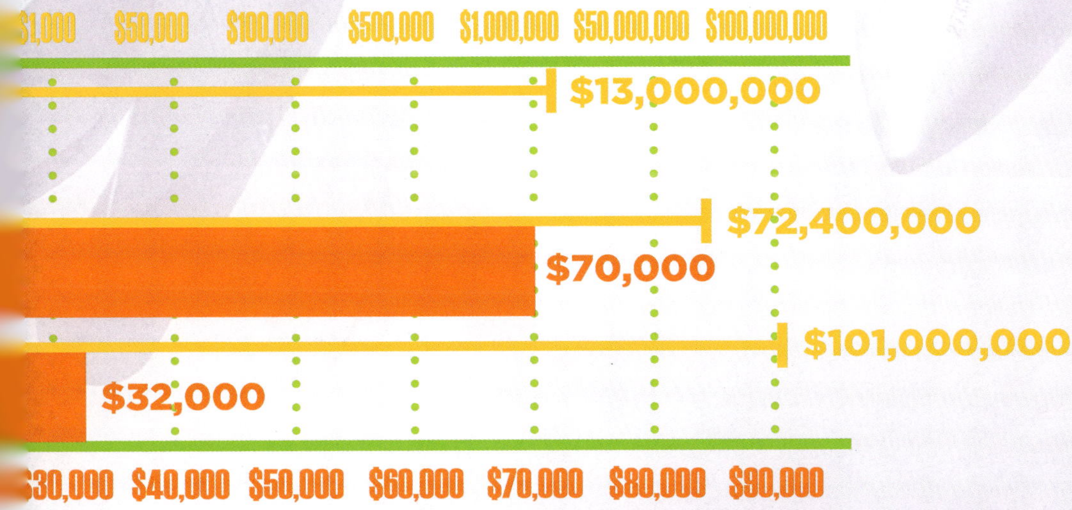

coating (KO-ting)—a thin layer or covering

drone (DROHN)—an unmanned aircraft or ship guided by remote control or onboard computer

mission (MISH-uhn)—a job assigned to a soldier

radar (RAY-dar)—a device that sends out radio waves for finding the location and speed of a moving object

refuel (ree-FEWL)—to add fuel

rotor (RO-tuhr)—spinning horizontal blades that support a helicopter in the air

stable (STAY-buhl)—steady or firm

stealth (STELTH)—an aircraft design that is hard for radar to pick up

supersonic (soo-pur-SON-ik)—faster than the speed of sound; the speed of sound is about 761 miles (1,225 km) per hour.

BOOKS

Cohn, Jessica. *Military Machines.* Machines in Motion. New York: Gareth Stevens Pub., 2014.

Gray, Judy Silverstein, and Taylor Baldwin Kiland. *Drones: Remote-Controlled Warfare.* Military Engineering in Action. New York: Enslow Publishing, 2016.

Murray, Aaron R. *Modern Military Aircraft.* What's Inside? New York: Sandy Creek, 2014.

WEBSITES

B-2 Spirit
www.af.mil/AboutUs/FactSheets/Display/tabid/224/Article/104482/b-2-spirit.aspx

Eurofighter Typhoon: The Aircraft
www.eurofighter.com/the-aircraft

ONE OF A KIND US Military V 22 Osprey Tiltrotor Aircraft
www.youtube.com/watch?v=hUNJTAybCQQ

INDEX